THE STATIONS OF THE CROSS

THE STATIONS OF THE CROSS

A Biblical Way

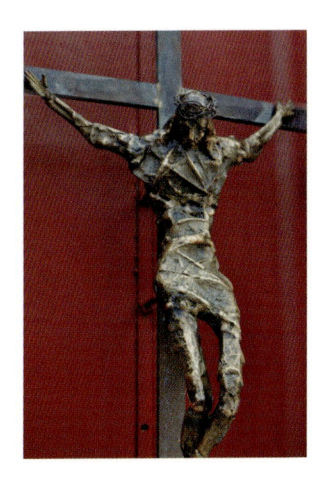

KIERAN HILL

VERITAS

First published 2013 by
Veritas Publications
7–8 Lower Abbey Street
Dublin 1
publications@veritas.ie
www.veritas.ie

Copyright © Kieran Hill, 2013
Photographs of Stations © Colleen McQuade, 2013

ISBN 978 1 84730 512 1

10 9 8 7 6 5 4 3 2 1

A catalogue record for this book is available
from the British Library.

Designed by Colette Dower, Veritas
Printed in the Republic of Ireland by Hudson Killeen Ltd, Dublin

Veritas books are printed on paper made from the wood pulp of managed forests. For every tree felled, at least one tree is planted, thereby renewing natural resources.

CONTENTS

Note from the Author	7
Foreword	9
The Stations of the Cross at Tobar Mhuire	11
How to pray and meditate on the Stations of the Cross	13

The First Station	Jesus in the Garden of Gethsemane	14
The Second Station	Jesus, betrayed by Judas, is arrested	16
The Third Station	Jesus is condemned by the Sanhedrin	18
The Fourth Station	Jesus is denied by Peter	20
The Fifth Station	Jesus is judged by Pilate	22
The Sixth Station	Jesus is scourged and crowned with thorns	24
The Seventh Station	Jesus bears the Cross	26
The Eighth Station	Jesus is helped by Simon the Cyrenian to carry the Cross	28
The Ninth Station	Jesus meets the Women	30
The Tenth Station	Jesus is crucified	32
The Eleventh Station	Jesus promises his Kingdom to the Good Thief	34

The Twelfth Station	Jesus speaks to his Mother and the Disciple	36
The Thirteenth Station	Jesus dies on the Cross	38
The Fourteenth Station	Jesus is placed in the Tomb	40
The Fifteenth Station	Jesus is risen from the Dead	42

About the Stations of the Cross,
Passionist Retreat Centre, Crossgar   44

NOTE FROM THE AUTHOR

The Passion of Christ is central to Passionist spirituality. The reflections offered in this booklet try to bring out Passionist themes as we journey with Jesus through his suffering, death and Resurrection. The Stations used in the booklet are those created by the Dublin artist Brian Byrne and newly installed at Tobar Mhuire. They follow the biblical Stations as introduced by Pope John Paul II in 1991.

Thanks is owed to Fr John Friel CP, Rector, for his assistance in developing this booklet and for permission to include images from Tobar Mhuire. Appreciation is also extended to Very Rev. Patrick Duffy CP, Provincial, and to other members of the Passionist Community at Tobar Mhuire; Fr Austin McGirr, PP Portstewart; Brian Quinn, architect, for his commentary and photograph included at the back of the booklet; and to Colleen McQuade for the photographs of the Stations of the Cross.

FOREWORD

Saint Paul of the Cross (1694–1775) founded the Congregation of the Passion of Jesus Christ, the Passionists, whose call was to promote the memory of the Passion. The journey to Golgotha is filled with suffering, pain, brokenness, sadness and fear, ending in physical death for Jesus. Saint Paul of the Cross had experienced much sadness with the death of ten of his brothers and sisters in childhood. These, and other life events, served to reinforce his belief in God's compassion and his transforming presence when we meditate and remember Christ's Passion. He wrote:

> The Passion of Our Lord Jesus Christ is the greatest and most admirable proof of God's love.

Saint Paul of the Cross believed in the active and constant presence of God in all situations, even those where this presence is not immediately evident. During his Passion, Jesus stayed with his suffering, placing complete trust in the loving care of his Father. For those who witnessed in their heart the mystery of Christ's suffering, death and Resurrection, God's transforming presence, love and compassion were manifest.

Passionists keep the memory of Christ's Passion alive in today's world, their mission summarised succinctly in their emblem. The heart and white cross represent the love of God. The inscription comes in the three traditional biblical languages:

> JESU   Hebrew for Jesus
> XPI   Greek for 'Christ' (shortened form) and
> PASSIO Latin for Passion.

This emblem is unique to the Passionist Community at Crossgar, and includes a Celtic knot, symbolising God's eternal love – no beginning and no end.

THE STATIONS OF THE CROSS AT TOBAR MHUIRE

The Passionists acquired Tobar Mhuire in 1950, relocating its Juniorate (a school for boys interested in joining the Passionist Religious life) from its Wheatfield site in North Belfast. The school closed in 1980 but in 1982, in addition to a Novitiate to help in the formation of those determining their vocation to Religious life, Tobar Mhuire was developed as a Retreat and Prayer Centre.

A major renovation and redesign of Tobar Mhuire was completed in 2012, during which time the Stations of the Cross were designed and erected in the chapel courtyard. Fabricated in the form of universal steel columns, fourteen Stations are finished in Passion colours, with each Station bearing a bronze carving representing one of the relevant Passion scenes as recorded in the Gospels and introduced by Pope John Paul II in 1991. The fifteenth Station, 'Jesus is risen from the Dead', is finished in white.

The Stations, as referenced in the Gospels, are:
I. Jesus in the Garden of Gethsemane
II. Jesus, betrayed by Judas, is arrested
III. Jesus is condemned by the Sanhedrin
IV. Jesus is denied by Peter
V. Jesus is judged by Pilate

VI. Jesus is scourged and crowned with thorns
VII. Jesus bears the Cross
VIII. Jesus is helped by Simon the Cyrenian to carry the Cross
IX. Jesus meets the Women
X. Jesus is crucified

XI. Jesus promises his Kingdom to the Good Thief
XII. Jesus speaks to his Mother and the Disciple
XIII. Jesus dies on the Cross
XIV. Jesus is placed in the Tomb
XV. Jesus is risen from the Dead

We journey through the Stations, connecting with Christ on his journey to Calvary. By praying, meditating and remembering in our hearts the pain and suffering of Jesus, may we be able to experience the transforming presence of God's love and compassion in our lives today and be strengthened in the hope that is the Resurrection.

HOW TO PRAY AND MEDITATE ON THE STATIONS OF THE CROSS

Opening Prayer

Dear Jesus,
I come to remember you in my heart,
to spend this time in prayer and meditation
as I walk, in step with your steps, towards Golgotha.
Help me to ponder in my heart the mystery of your
suffering and pain, which you endured for my salvation,
and to experience the love, compassion and mercy of
God, our Father.
Amen.

Genuflect at each Stations saying:
V. **We adore you, O Christ, and we praise you**
R. **Because by your holy cross, you have redeemed the world.**

Read each reflection slowly, allowing words, thoughts and feelings to sink into your heart.

After each station say:

> **Our Father …**
> **Hail Mary …**
> **Glory be to the Father …**
>
> **Holy Mother, pierce me through,**
> **in my heart each wound renew**
> **of my Saviour Crucified.**
>
> **May the Passion of Jesus**
> **be always in our hearts.**

THE FIRST STATION
JESUS IN THE GARDEN OF GETHSEMANE

V. We adore you, O Christ, and we praise you
R. Because by your holy cross, you have redeemed the world.

As darkness descends, Gethsemane offers a place for peaceful prayer. Jesus enters with his disciples. He gathers Peter, James and John and takes them deeper into the garden. They are requested to:

> Remain • Watch • Pray.

Starlit stillness is broken as Jesus falls to earth. Body, mind and soul are tormented as Jesus experiences great sorrow and unbearable anguish.

Pleading for the cup of suffering to pass, the intensity of prayer is visible, as perspiration falls to earth like drops of blood. Bodily death is possible but not now. Not in this place. Jesus trusts his Father's love and totally submits to his will. Prayer is answered:

> Fear dissolved • Heavenly strength received • Stillness and resolve restored.

Peter, James and John, in their bodily weakness, are not yet fully open to the loving presence of God's compassion and mercy, present in the mystery of their master's suffering. They, like us, are drawn deeper and reminded to:

> Remain • Watch • Pray.

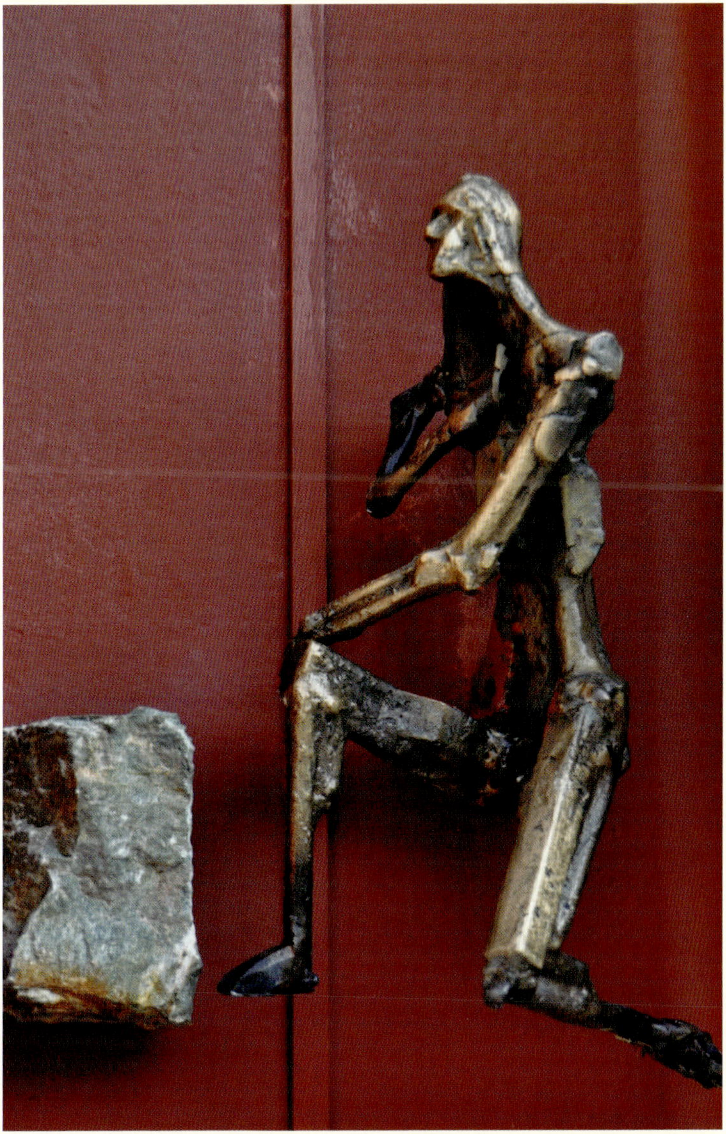

THE SECOND STATION
JESUS, BETRAYED BY JUDAS, IS ARRESTED

V. We adore you, O Christ, and we praise you
R. Because by your holy cross, you have redeemed the world.

Jesus wakes the weak, announcing he is betrayed. The disciples stir from their drowsiness as lighted torches reveal the face of one of their own, Judas, who is not alone. A crowd, commissioned by the chief priests, scribes and elders, fall in behind him. They, too, are seeking Jesus; darkness of the hour not able to hide the darkness of their intent:

Swords • Clubs.

Judas stands before Jesus and greets his master. A kiss, a sign of love and friendship, now used to sign an arrest. Jesus is to be seized by force; removed from his embrace with Judas. Jesus is betrayed.

Resistance calmed • Jesus stands firm • Suffering accepted.

Jesus is surrendering without a fight and the disciples are confused and fearful. Unable to see God's purpose they plan their own retreat. Jesus is deserted in his hour of need. In this moment of betrayal, become aware of God's planning, compassion and love for Jesus. Receive strength to:

Be calm • Stand firm • Accept.

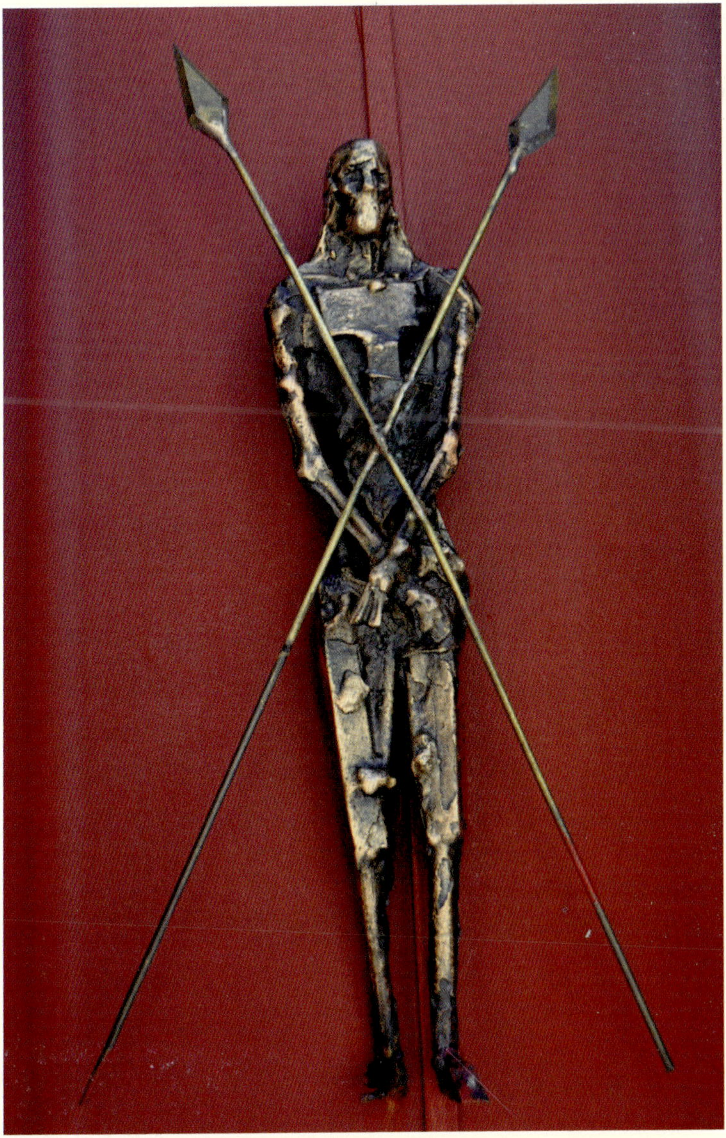

THE THIRD STATION
JESUS IS CONDEMNED BY THE SANHEDRIN

V. We adore you, O Christ, and we praise you
R. Because by your holy cross, you have redeemed the world.

Day breaks and Jesus is brought before the Sanhedrin, the Jewish council, headed by the high priest. Court convened, interrogators ready, the case against Jesus is backed by false testimony. Jesus shows no resistance and the court quickly get down to the core issue: does Jesus claim to be the Messiah? Jesus is fully aware of his situation. Speaking the truth, to those who do not believe, will lead to his conviction; defending himself will not change their minds. He appears to be in an impossible situation but retains the strength and conviction to declare:

Son of Man • To be seated at the right hand of God • Son of God.

The high priest demonstrates disgust as he tears his robes, the court declaring:

Blasphemy • Guilt • Death.

Truth rejected, Jesus is unjustly condemned. Remain with Jesus in this moment of false accusation as he looks to a more compassionate and merciful Judge who:

Hears truth • Declares innocence • Gives life.

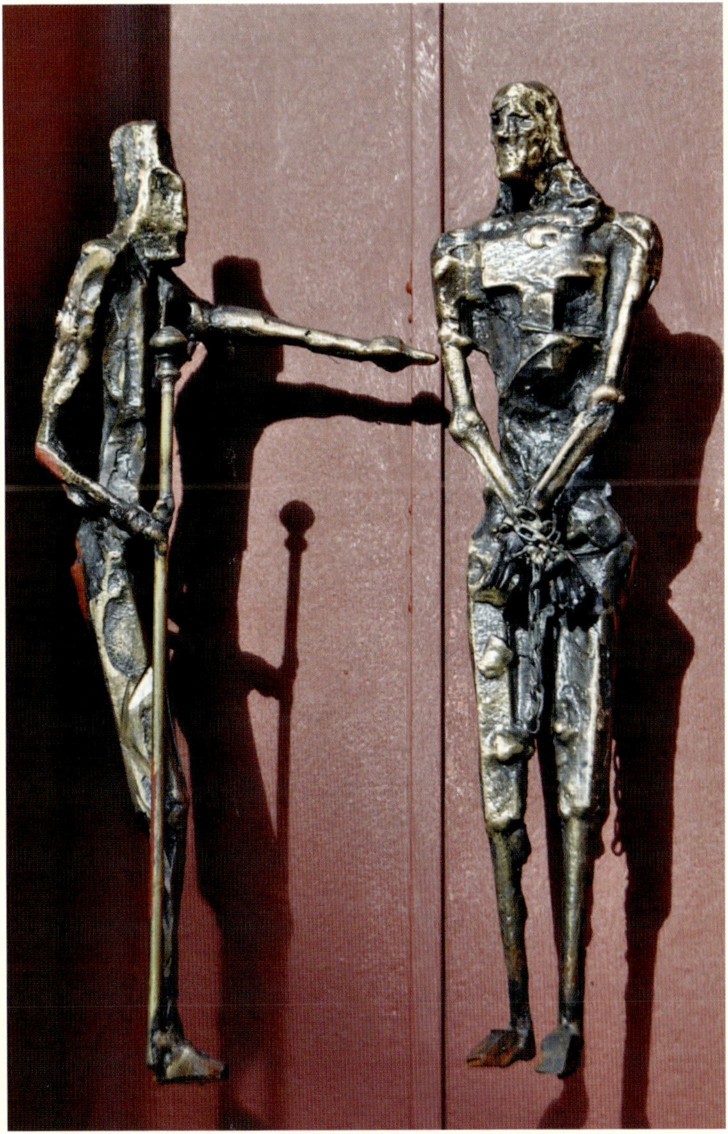

THE FOURTH STATION
JESUS IS DENIED BY PETER

V. We adore you, O Christ, and we praise you
R. Because by your holy cross, you have redeemed the world.

Peter follows, a distance behind. At the house of the high priest he finds the crowd gathered around a courtyard fire.

> Peter stops • Joins the crowd • Warms himself by the fire.

A servant girl approaches. She stares at Peter. The truth in her statement, that Peter follows Jesus, inwardly recognised by Peter but outwardly denied to those around him. Jesus, the one who:

> Chose Peter • Remained with Peter • Loved Peter – is now renounced by Peter.

Peter moves away. His plight in pursuit as a further challenge is voiced. He again denies any knowledge of Jesus. Safe for the moment, but then an even stronger accusation points Peter out to the crowd. Peter, the 'Rock', crumbles as courage deserts him. The level of his denial raised to match that of the accusation. A cock crows; the sharp sound piercing his memory, echoing the words of Jesus' prediction:

> Denial • Three times • Cock will crow – Peter weeps bitterly.

Remain with Peter as courage deserts him, denial of Jesus is repeated and bitter tears of regret and repentance flow. Courage will return to continue walking with Jesus.

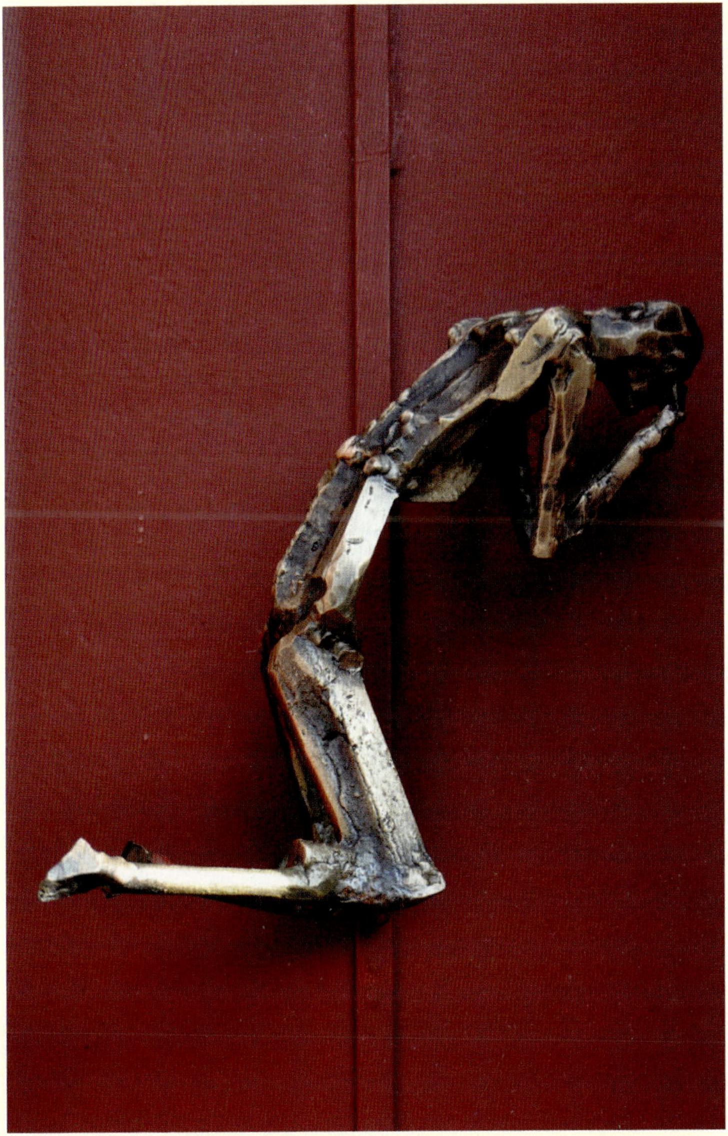

THE FIFTH STATION
JESUS IS JUDGED BY PILATE

V. We adore you, O Christ, and we praise you
R. Because by your holy cross, you have redeemed the world.

It is now morning. The decision to hand Jesus over has been made and he is brought, bound, to Pilate. Jesus stands before Roman authority; power over life and death in Pilate's hands. Pilate questions: 'King of the Jews?' Jesus speaks of heavenly authority, his Kingdom not of this world. Remaining close to his Father and the purpose of his mission, Jesus offers no defence. Silence. Pilate pleads to the crowd:

> No guilt found • Death not deserved • Release Jesus?

The crowd, prompted by the chief priests, are stirred to respond:

> Guilt found • Death deserved • Crucify Jesus!

The crowd's shouts are heard. Barabbas, who is guilty, being preferred for release over Jesus, who is innocent. Inwardly judging Jesus to be innocent but outwardly condemning him to death creates conflict for Pilate. Washing his hands in public, removing any prompting for tears of regret or repentance for this injustice.

Remain with Jesus in his silence as Pilate, to relieve his own conflict, requests his release, and the crowd shouts for crucifixion. Unlike Pilate and the crowd, may we:

> Accept the truth of Jesus' divine majesty.
> In difficult times, feel God's compassion, mercy and hope.

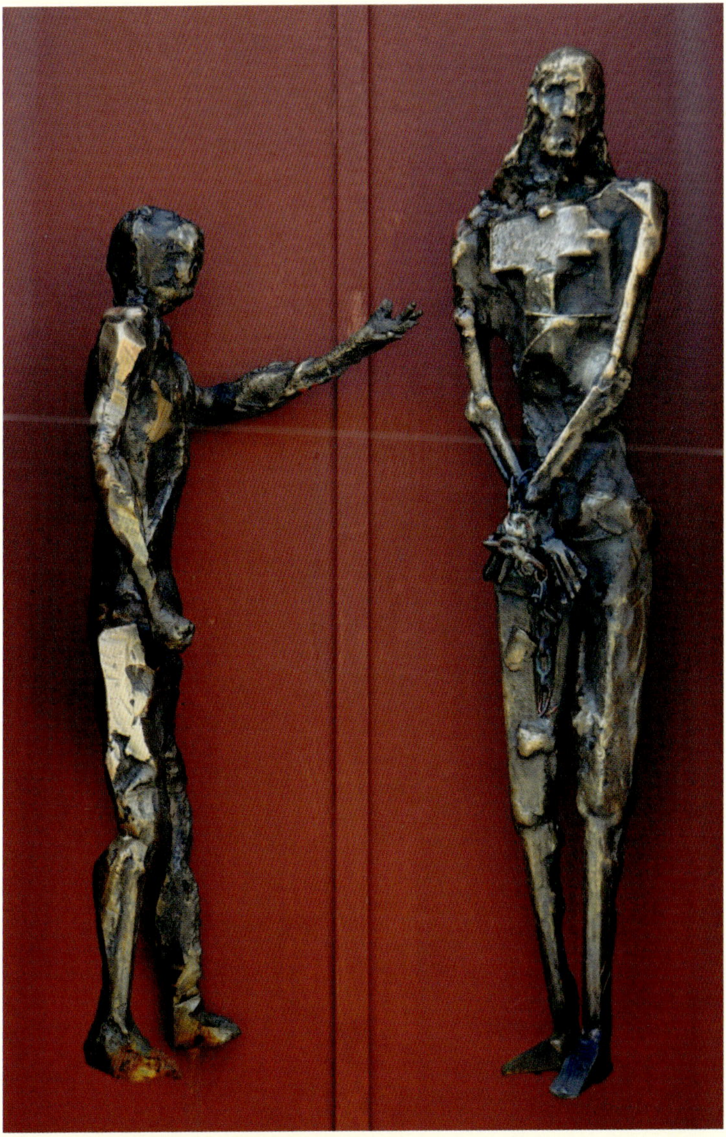

THE SIXTH STATION
JESUS IS SCOURGED AND CROWNED WITH THORNS

V. We adore you, O Christ, and we praise you
R. Because by your holy cross, you have redeemed the world.

Pilate orders Jesus to be scourged. Stripped of his clothes and bound, Jesus endures the punishment without complaint. His body, offered with compassion to his Apostles a few hours previously, now returns to Pilate bearing deep stripes of suffering mercilessly inflicted.

The suffering continues as Jesus is brought before hundreds of Roman soldiers. Stripped again of his clothes Jesus is, with ridicule, robed in scarlet as a 'king', a reed sceptre placed in his right hand and a crown of twisted thorns pressed on his head.

The soldiers kneel and acclaim Jesus 'King of the Jews'. The mockery of their actions obvious by the insults, spit and repeated blows directed at Jesus. Emotions roused by the humiliating and degrading treatment rather than an awareness of the true 'Kingship' of the one they mock.

Remain with Jesus as he endures this physical and emotional pain. Unlike the Roman soldiers and crowd may we:

> Look more deeply at Jesus.
> Feel compassion.
> See his Divine Majesty.
> Accept, with gratitude, his deep suffering.
> Let his love heal our wounds.

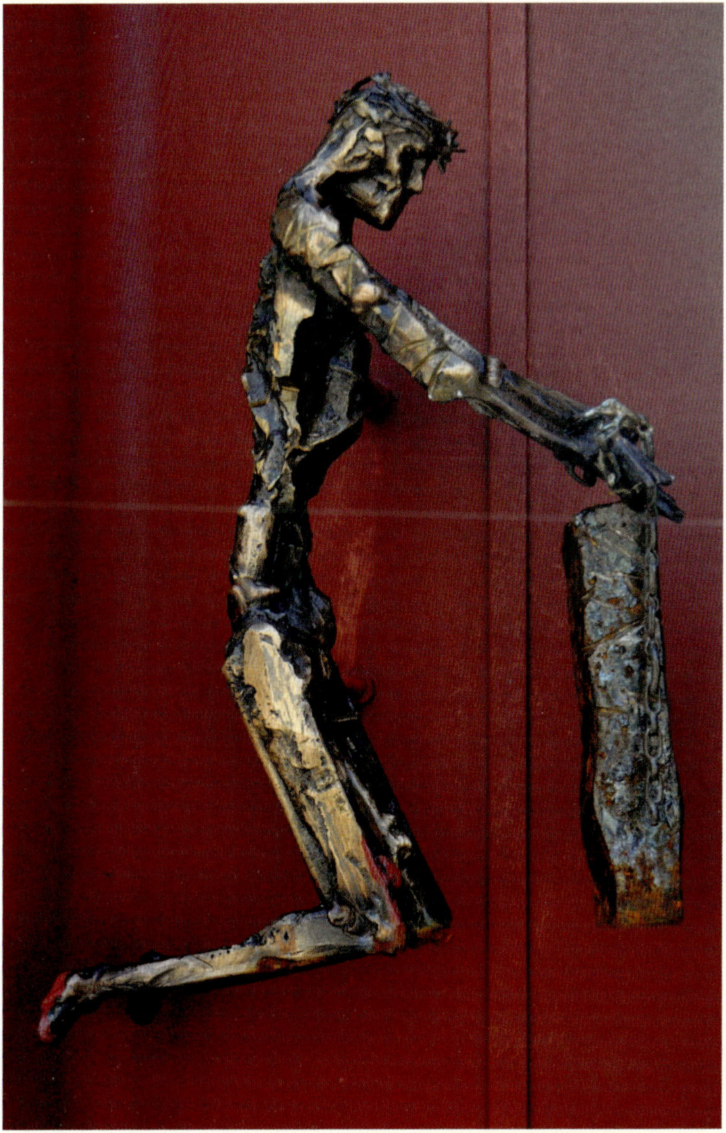

THE SEVENTH STATION
JESUS BEARS THE CROSS

V. We adore you, O Christ, and we praise you
R. Because by your holy cross, you have redeemed the world.

Jesus takes up the cross. Wood, once upright, breathing, clothed and shaped for beauty, now cut down, breathless, stripped back and shaped for a different purpose – Pilate's punishment. Despite being weakened by whips, Jesus summons sufficient strength to take his first steps towards Golgotha.

Weighed down by the enormity of the burden, it is a difficult journey, but love strengthens his grip. Roman soldiers force the procession through the crowds.

>Jesus must reach Golgotha alive.
>The sentence must be carried out.
>Jesus knows what is required.
>He trusts his Father.
>He will reach Golgotha.

Embracing the cross, Jesus carries on. Sometimes our own cross is difficult. Too heavy to carry alone. Sometimes we summon our own 'crowd' or 'Roman soldiers' to keep it distant or to block God's love. Look again! Remain with Jesus as he struggles to carry the cross to Golgotha.

Share his burden • Witness love in action • Continue along the right path.

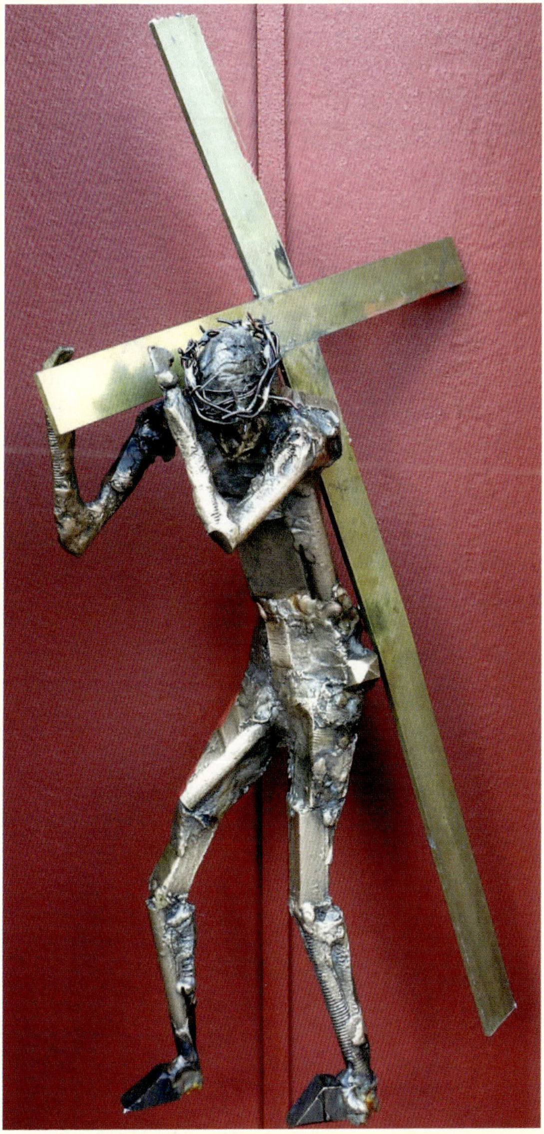

THE EIGHTH STATION
JESUS IS HELPED BY SIMON THE CYRENIAN TO CARRY THE CROSS

V. We adore you, O Christ, and we praise you
R. Because by your holy cross, you have redeemed the world.

Jesus is weak and exhausted. He struggles to carry the cross through Jerusalem's streets and out of the gates towards Golgotha. At another time Jesus had been lifted up and carried into the city on a donkey adorned; leaves and branches waving as the crowd shouted 'Hosanna'.

Now the crowds gather again: Passover pilgrims, spectators, participants and those just passing a painful and sorrowful procession. They witness Jesus lifting up and carrying the wood of the cross, unadorned. Arms of the crowds waving to very different shouts.

A man from Cyrene, having journeyed in from the country, finds himself singled out. Seized by soldiers, Simon is compelled to help Jesus carry the cross. Forced to connect, through the wood of the cross, to the suffering Jesus. The road to Golgotha is difficult but Jesus is walking ahead, leading the way. Simon follows the footsteps of Jesus.

Jesus walks the path to Golgotha knowing that his Father walks with him and that there is a redeeming purpose to his suffering. Like Simon, let us:

Walk behind Jesus • Touch the cross • Feel Jesus touching our lives.

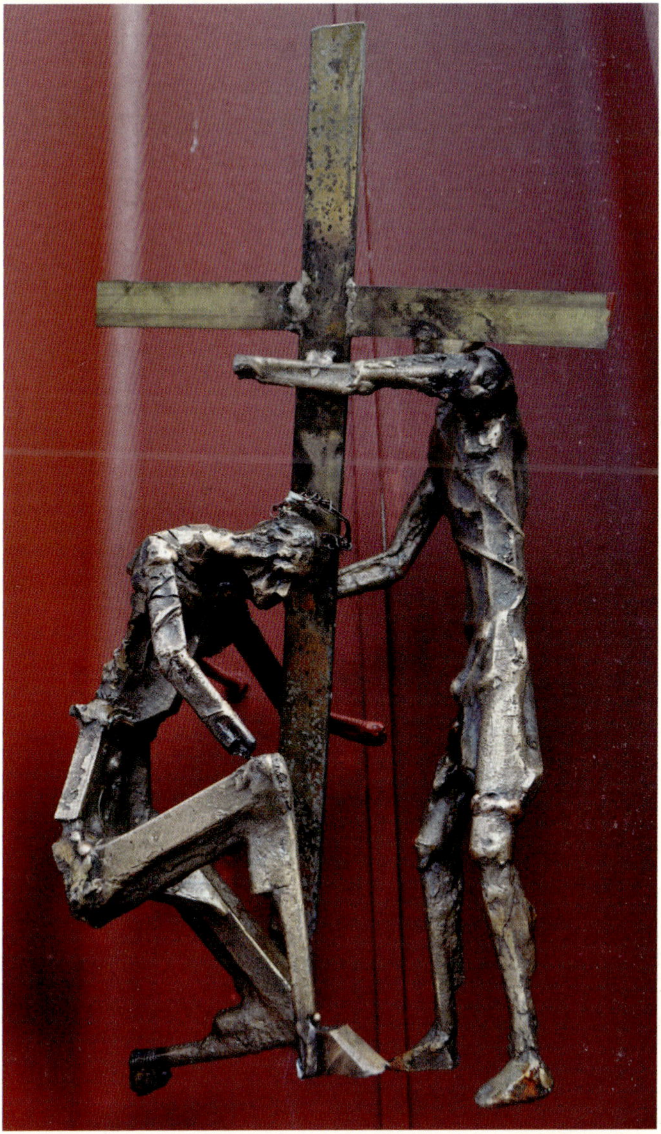

THE NINTH STATION
JESUS MEETS THE WOMEN

V. We adore you, O Christ, and we praise you
R. Because by your holy cross, you have redeemed the world.

Crowds continue to follow behind Jesus as he painfully processes along the path to Golgotha. Women, gathered in grief, are unable to contain their distress and loudly weep at the sight of Jesus in his suffering. Without fear they let their voices be heard, their feelings known:

Jesus is not alone • Life has meaning • Compassion is shown.

Jesus turns to the women. In his sorrow Jesus understands their present pain which he requests they redirect: weep for themselves and their children. Tears linking two tragic moments in history.

This tragedy when: Jesus is walking among the people;
The wood is 'green';
Jesus is physically destroyed.
Future tragedy when: Jesus is not walking among the people;
The wood is 'dry';
Jerusalem is physically destroyed.

Power, blind to Jesus and his Father's love, compassion and mercy, delivers destruction. We know of many other 'Jerusalems' where tears continue to flow. The world needs life, 'green wood'. Jesus is the life of the world. We are children of our own 'Jerusalem'. Let us remain with Jesus as he is speaking to the women.

Listen to what he is saying.
Turn to where he is pointing – ourselves, family, city, country.
Feel comforted in the compassion of Jesus and his Father.

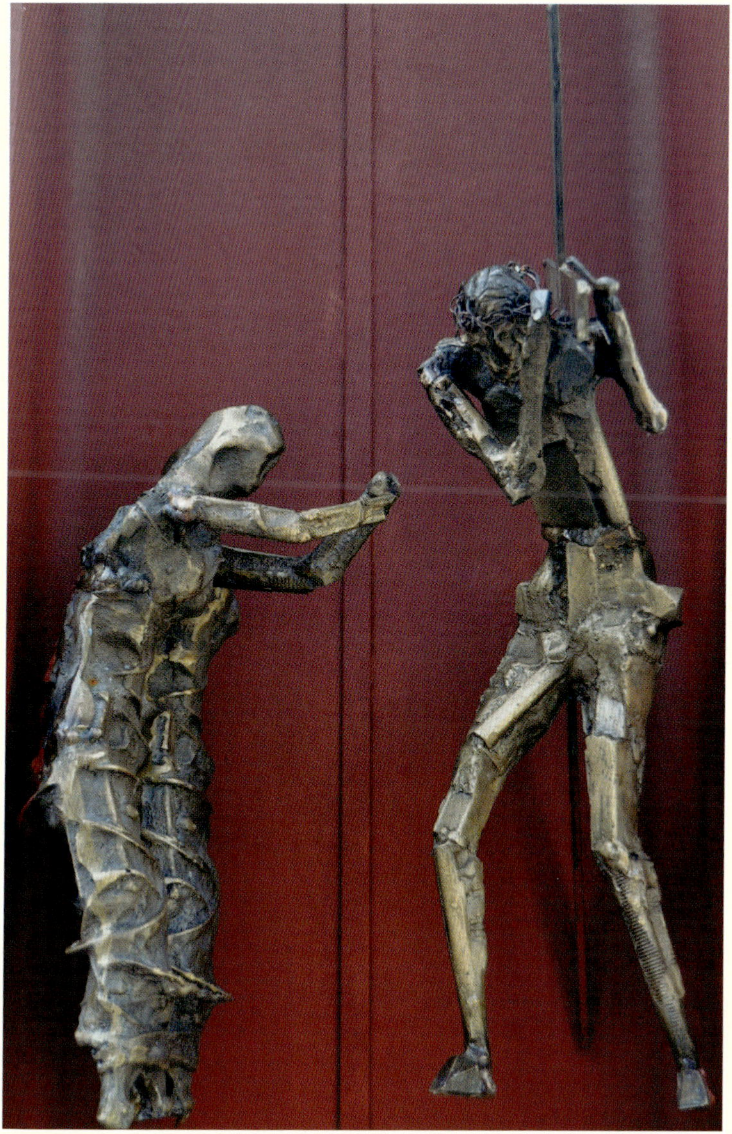

THE TENTH STATION
JESUS IS CRUCIFIED

V. We adore you, O Christ, and we praise you
R. Because by your holy cross, you have redeemed the world.

Jesus reaches Golgotha. When sin first came into the world, clothes were put on to hide shame. Now as redemption approaches, Jesus, the redeemer, is stripped of his clothes; shame left at the foot of the cross as the relationship with God is being restored.

Stripped wood now adorned as Jesus' hands and feet are nailed to the cross. The cross, which Pilate personalised in three languages, tells the world who it is that they are crucifying: 'Jesus of Nazareth. King of the Jews.'

Disbelief, insults and mockery continue as the crowd gaze up at Jesus. The true Messiah would not let this happen. He would come down from the cross and save himself and Jerusalem. If this happens then the crowd will believe. A final miracle is demanded. Jesus had worked miracles before and crowds had not believed. Love, not nails, keeps Jesus from accepting their challenge now.

Jesus came into the world to proclaim God's reign. He continues to place his trust in his Father as he asks for forgiveness to be given to those who crucify him. A miracle and mystery of perfect love. Remain looking at Jesus on the cross.

> Enter into the mystery of his suffering.
> Leave shame at the foot of the cross.
> Feel the compassion and restoring mercy of God.

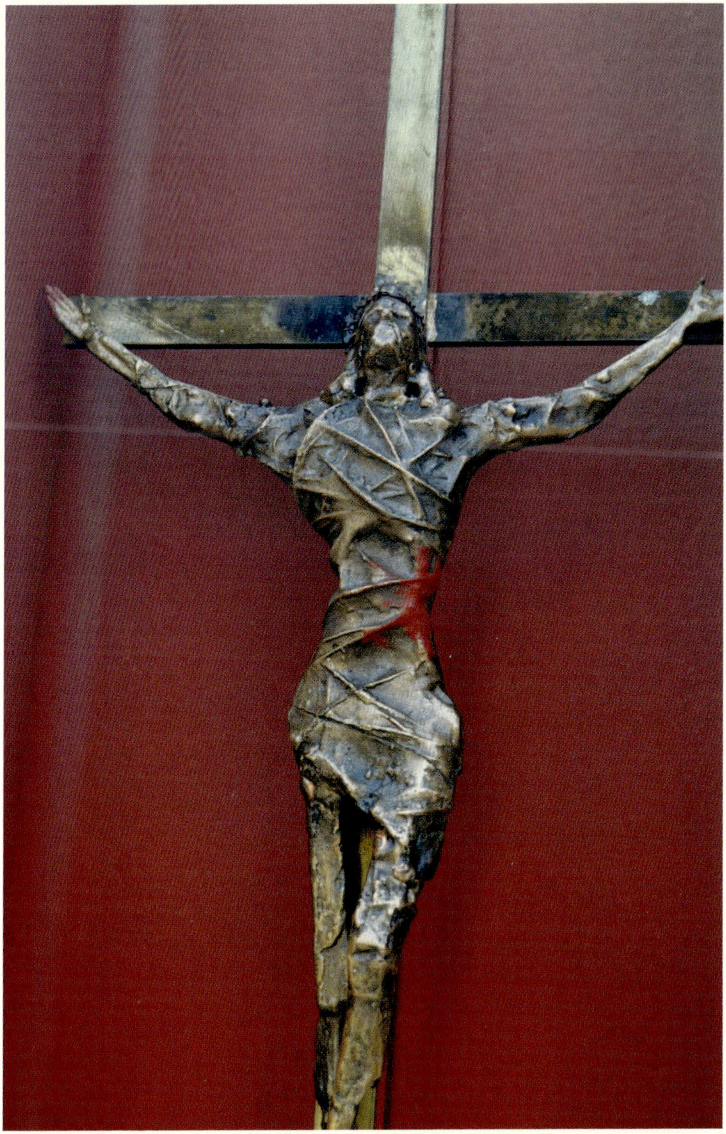

THE ELEVENTH STATION
JESUS PROMISES HIS KINGDOM TO THE GOOD THIEF

V. We adore you, O Christ, and we praise you
R. Because by your holy cross, you have redeemed the world.

Jesus is crucified with two other men. Convicted and sentenced to death, these men flank each side of Jesus as he hangs on the cross. One of the men mimics the shouts from the crowd and, abusing Jesus, questions him as to whether he is the Messiah and demands all three be saved.

The other condemned man responds, testifying that he and the other criminal are guilty, their punishment deserved, but that Jesus is innocent. A defence too late for earthly judgement, it is this man in his hour of death who speaks the truth.

Recognising Jesus' majesty, he asks to be permitted entry into Jesus' Kingdom, Pilate's notice on the cross pointing the way: upwards towards heaven. Reward is swift for such an act of faith and Jesus tells him they will meet that day in Paradise.

Reflect with Jesus as he faces two very different responses to suffering and death. Jesus offering salvation right up to the end of life.

> Remain with Jesus as he responds generously.
> Repent and receive the mercy and compassion of Jesus.
> Hear the promise of Paradise.

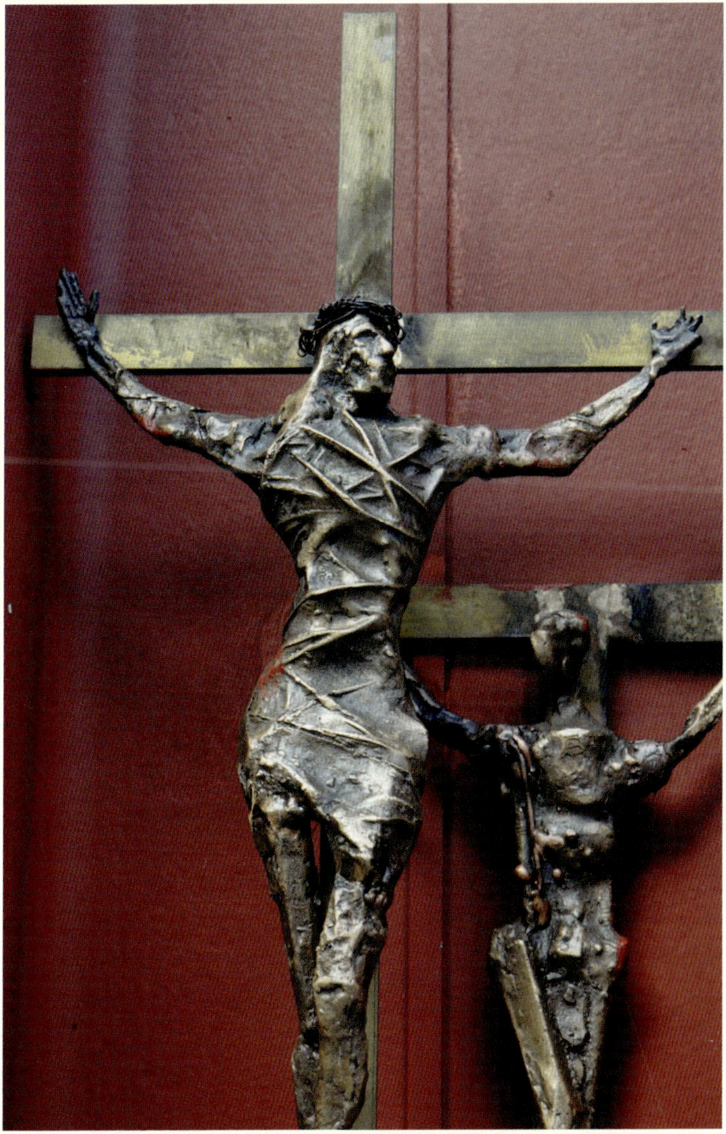

THE TWELFTH STATION
JESUS SPEAKS TO HIS MOTHER AND THE DISCIPLE

V. We adore you, O Christ, and we praise you
R. Because by your holy cross, you have redeemed the world.

With Jesus from his conception, Mary remains close to her Son in his last suffering as she stands beneath the cross, the prophetic words of Simeon truly evident in the pierced hands and feet of her Son now dying on the cross.

Her soul is pierced with sorrow.

The disciple whom Jesus loved is with Mary at the foot of the cross. He remains close to his master. Jesus looks at his Mother and the disciple. At this time of suffering his thoughts are on those who are to be left behind. He has something of great importance to say before he dies. Jesus makes his final wishes known:

Mary to accept the disciple as her Son.
The disciple to accept Mary as his Mother.
Mary to be taken into the disciple's home.

The bond, sealed in sorrow, will ensure Mary is given support to cope with the tremendous loss of her Son. She is given her place among the disciples and followers of Jesus. Mary continues to be close to those who follow her Son. Remain at the foot of the cross with Mary and the disciple.

Reflect on the emotions as Jesus speaks.
Let his words pierce our hearts, allowing compassion a gateway in.
Receive Mary as our Mother.

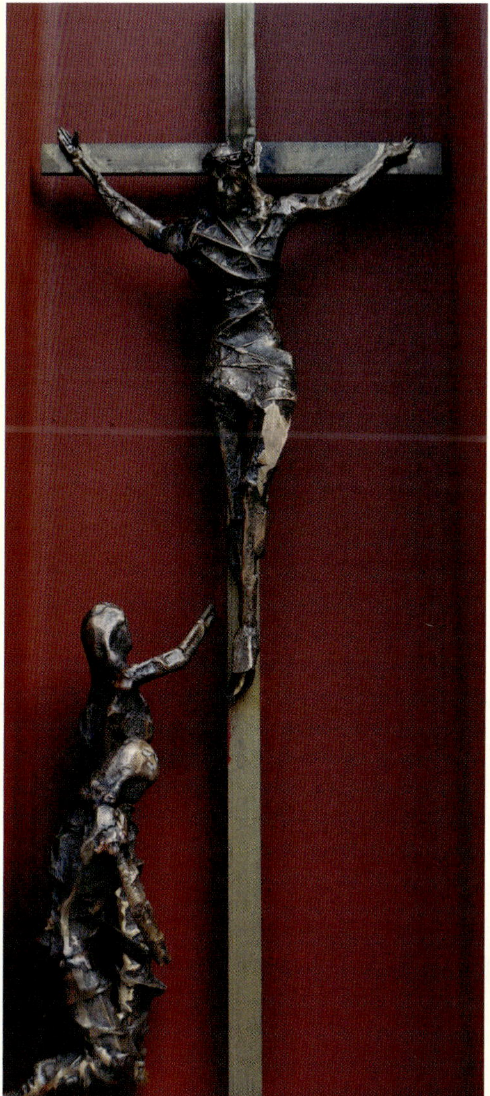

THE THIRTEENTH STATION
JESUS DIES ON THE CROSS

V. We adore you, O Christ, and we praise you
R. Because by your holy cross, you have redeemed the world.

Suffering is slow as Jesus remains on the cross. A star once shone brightly when Jesus came into the world. Now, for three hours, sunlight dims in recognition of his suffering. The Light of the World fades with each gasp for breath. It is painful to watch.

The crowds watch, some still curiously hoping to witness heavenly intervention from the prophet Elijah, even at this late stage. Elijah does not come. Jesus remains on the cross in obedience to his Father's will, struggling in his last moments of life.

The earth shakes as two great forces, death and redemption, battle it out for victory.

The Temple veil tears in two • Redemption wins • Separation from God ends.

Jesus speaks to let us know that his Father's work has been 'accomplished' before giving up his last breath. Remain with Jesus during his last moments. Become aware of God's compassion, love and mercy as Jesus, his Son, is offered in sacrifice.

Kneel: Jesus dying for our sins.
Pause: Jesus struggling with Death to win our Redemption.
Breathe: No greater love.

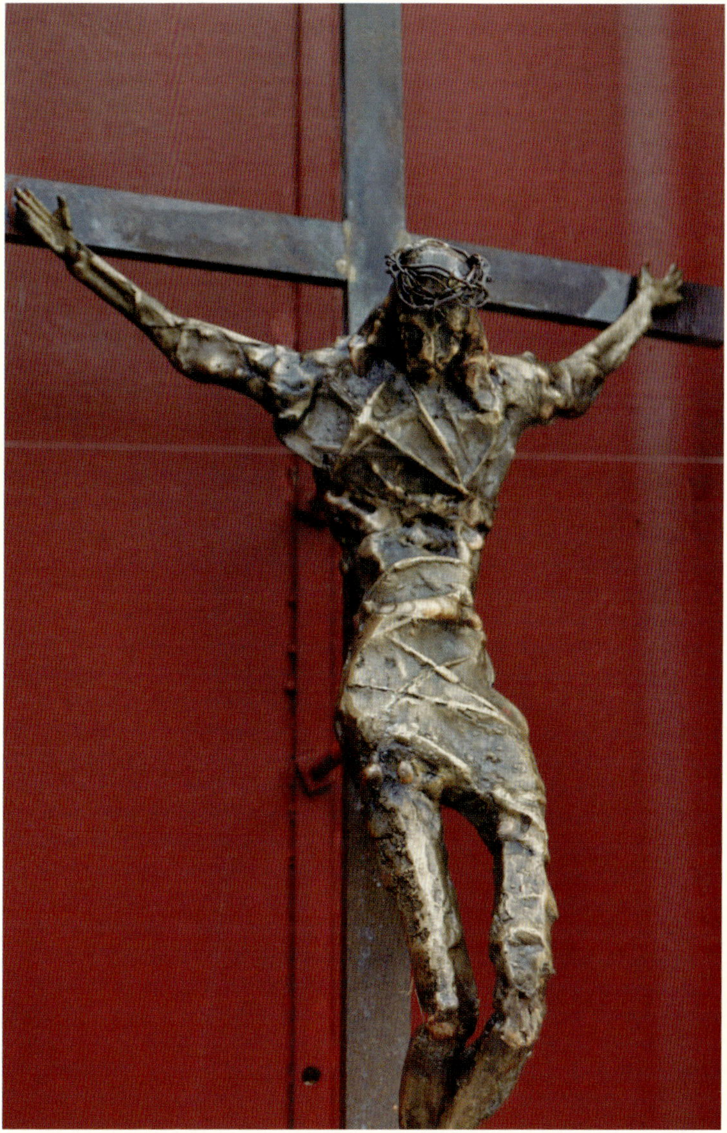

THE FOURTEENTH STATION
JESUS IS PLACED IN THE TOMB

V. We adore you, O Christ, and we praise you
R. Because by your holy cross, you have redeemed the world.

Not all of the Jewish council sought the death of Jesus. Joseph, a wealthy man from Arimathea, is a disciple and follower of Jesus. For those, like Joseph, whose expectations about the Messiah and the coming of the Kingdom were raised, the death of Jesus brings sadness, uncertainty and diminished hope.

Joseph takes bold and decisive action. Going directly to Pilate, he requests the body of Jesus be released to him. He knows what needs to be done, especially given the fast-approaching Sabbath.

> Jesus is taken down from the cross.
> His body, destroyed by violence, is at peace.
> Everything given up, the sacrifice complete.

There is little time to grieve, to say final farewells as Joseph wraps Jesus' body in a clean linen shroud in preparation for burial. Jesus, who earlier had carried the lifeless cross to Golgotha, is carried lifeless from Golgotha to a place of rest. Held in love, Jesus' body is treated with the utmost dignity and respect as it is laid in the tomb, hastily hewn from rock. Joseph secures the entrance of the tomb with a large stone. Woman followers observe where Jesus is laid to rest.

Remain in vigil at the tomb of Jesus. His restful body lies within.

A stone keeps Jesus apart • Soon this stone will be removed • Keep hope alive.

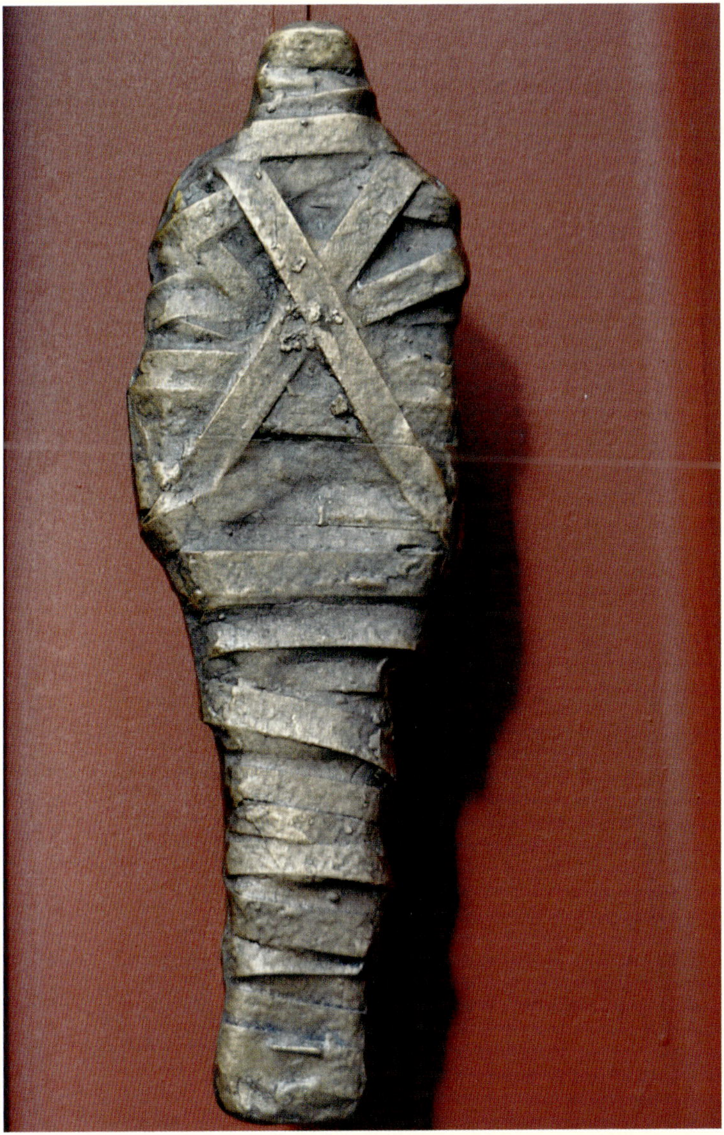

THE FIFTEENTH STATION
JESUS IS RISEN FROM THE DEAD

V. We adore you, O Christ, and we praise you
R. Because by your holy cross, you have redeemed the world.

Wishing to keep Jesus contained within his tomb, the chief priests and Pharisees convince Pilate to place a guard at its entrance. Early on the third day, Mary Magdalene and another woman go to the tomb of Jesus to anoint his body. The large stone has been rolled away, the tomb's entrance is open. No guards barring their way, the women go into the tomb. Shocked at not finding Jesus, the women are further startled when two men in 'dazzling' clothes join them in the tomb announcing:

> Jesus is not among the dead.
> Jesus is Risen.

The Apostles find it just as difficult to believe when the women recount what they have seen. Peter and another disciple rush to the tomb to check with their own eyes what their ears have heard. They find only the white burial cloths within. Could it be true? Jesus has risen from the dead? The other disciple begins to believe.

We, too, sometimes find it difficult to see through pain, suffering and death to the Resurrection experience. We remain stuck at the cross unable, or unwilling, to move on. Remain at the empty tomb. Light shines out to show that our redemption requires resurrection. May we too be startled so as to believe:

> Jesus is no longer among the dead.
> Jesus is alive.
> Hope is restored.

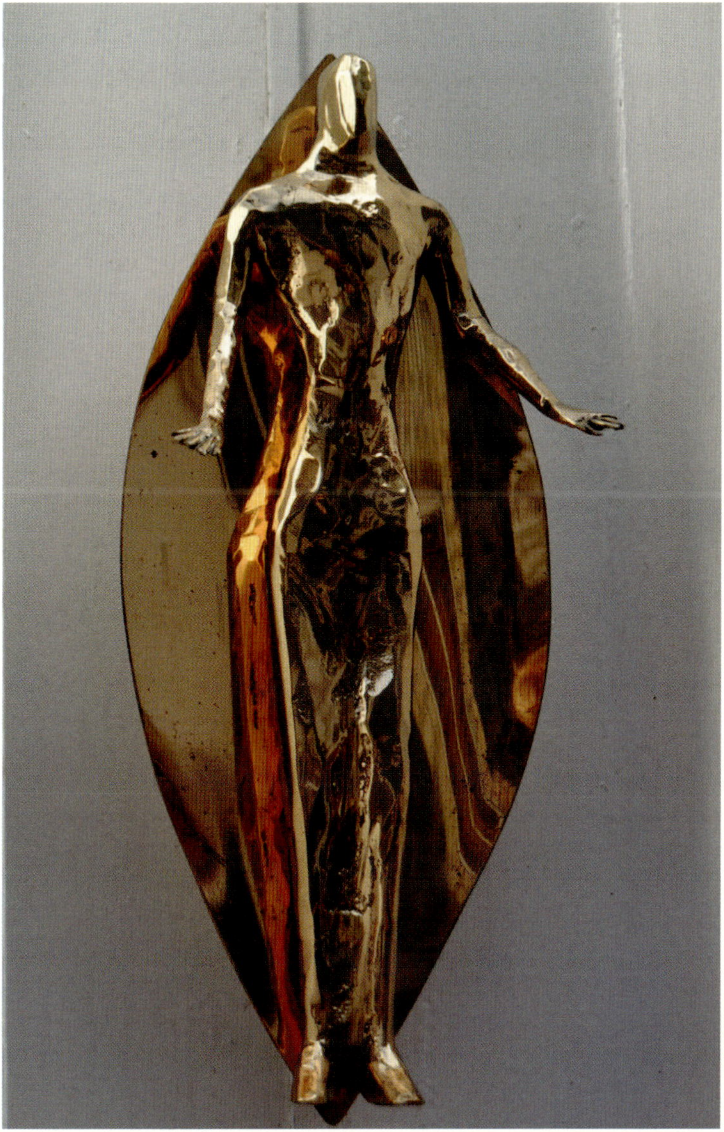

ABOUT THE STATIONS OF THE CROSS, PASSIONIST RETREAT CENTRE, CROSSGAR

'Tobar Mhuire' means 'Mary's Well' in Irish and is the name of the monastery established in 1950 by the Passionist Congregation in Crossgar, Co. Down, Northern Ireland.

In 2010 the Congregation decided to refurbish the monastery to become a retreat and outreach centre suitable for the twenty-first century. The refurbishment included liturgical changes to the chapel and the commissioning of new Stations of the Cross by the Irish artist Brian Byrne.

The spirituality of the Passionist Congregation has at its centre the Passion, death and Resurrection of Jesus Christ and an engagement with meditation on the Passion to spread the Gospel and transform the secular world. The new Stations of the Cross had to express this spirituality and mission. This was to be achieved by their location within the monastery and by their design.

It was decided to place them outside in the central courtyard at the entrance to the chapel. The courtyard thus becomes a sculpture court with a new meaning and function, the scene for a personal encounter with the Passion. The Stations are thus at the centre of the monastery, literally and metaphorically.

The Stations are three-dimensional figures cast in bronze and mounted on fifteen steel stanchions. They are visceral, raw and immediate, confronting and demanding a new interaction between the Passion and the viewer. They are arranged so that the road to

Golgotha can be followed individually and repeatedly, terminating at the entrance to the chapel with the fifteenth station, Jesus is risen from the Dead.

In the courtyard the Stations are freed from the liturgical hierarchy of the chapel and are located at the spatial heart of the monastery itself, silent but not mute witnesses to the greatest act of love ever known.

Brian Quinn, Architect

Photograph courtesy of Brian Quinn